"What you do, the way you think, makes you beautiful."

—Scott Westerfeld

I Like My Body

A 52 – Week Journal To Honor and Appreciate My Body

From the author of 'Body Shame BS,' Plus Size Cover Model and Body Acceptance Coach

Dr. Felicia Clark

I Like My Body
A 52 – Week Journal To Honor And Appreciate My Body

iUniverse books may be ordered through booksellers or by contacting:

iUniverse LLC
1663 Liberty Drive
Bloomington, IN 47403
www.iuniverse.com
1-800-Authors (1-800-288-4677)

Because of the dynamic nature of the Internet, any web addresses or links contained in this book may have changed since publication and may no longer be valid. The views expressed in this work are solely those of the author and do not necessarily reflect the views of the publisher, and the publisher hereby disclaims any responsibility for them.

ISBN: 978-1-4917-3473-5 (sc)
ISBN: 978-1-4917-3474-2 (e)

Printed in the United States of America.

Contents

Introduction:

Over 80% of girls and women dislike their body in some way. That is, in part, because females are taught far more negative and defeating beliefs about their body than positive messages. Often, these negative messages come from advertisers trying to shame us into buying their products and from women who compete for beauty.

Did you know that ___every___ part of the female body (including inside) has a thriving industry financially dependent on improving or "fixing" what isn't broken? They can make you to feel broken so that you become a repeat beauty customer trying to purge that broken feeling. They use sales tactics that teach you that your natural looks and smells are inadequate and keeping you from the life of your dreams. "Behind every woman's insecurity is a billion dollar shaming industry," says Dr. Felicia Clark, author of **_Body Shame BS: 7-Steps To Overcome The Big Business of Low Self-Esteem._** The result of receiving multiple negative body image "fix it" messages every day, can be body disconnect or even body hatred. This journal helps you practice what it looks and feels like to make beauty decisions in the spirit of joy instead of complying with other people's beauty standards. If you were taught to dislike your body in any way, you can be taught to like your body – forever. Join the online interactive journal community at www.BodyShameBS.com to learn healthy beauty practices, model secrets, and get ideas on how to complete your journal.

Do you know if you are using beauty practices that poison and harm your body? Are you considering getting risky and painful procedures done to your body? What if the way you feel about yourself, not your physical appearance, is holding you back? What if your body is miraculous the way it is now?

Over the next year, this journal will guide you through Dr. Felicia Clark's 7-step process of mind, body, spirit connection previously only available to her private coaching clients. Dr. Clark, a plus size cover model, is one of the nation's leading body acceptance coaches for women.

Here is Dr. Clark's 7-step process that you will undergo in this journal each week:
1) Choose a part of your body, decide to like it, and give it special treatment for the week.
2) Learn the purpose of that part of your body.
3) Chose 1 or more things that you like about that part of your body.
4) Choose or refuse to put that part of your body into beauty service for others while choosing healthier or harmless grooming practices.
5) Speak positively to and about that part of your body. Give it a positive name and slogan.
6) Decide how you will remind yourself to like that part of your body if negative messages creep back in.
7) Thank that part of your body in a letter and commit to how you will take care of it in the future using healthy products and grooming regimens.

To get the most out of your journal, apply these tips:
- Don't overthink it.
- You can write the same thing for multiple days or something different each day.
- NO NEGATIVITY! No buts as in "I like my eyes but…"
- Go out of order if you get stuck.

- Change or skip the weekly topic if it does not apply to you.
- Search online to help you complete the journal (example: "the purpose of hair") or enroll in the online course at www.BodyShameBS.com to get ideas.
- Use the compliments that other people have given you in the box for "positive vibe/slogan."
- If you want to be creative, write a poem each week in place of the letter to your body.
- It is best to complete a journal entry each day. If everyday doesn't work, complete the entry for all 7 days at the beginning of the week and post in on your bathroom mirror.
- Have fun!
- If you fail to complete a week, still move on to the next week to appreciate another part of your body.
- Chose a consistent time to complete your journal (e.g. when you wake up, during lunch, before bed, etc.).
- Use different color pens or fonts.
- Complete the journal with a friend or in a group.
- Attend a live event or teleseminar by Dr. Clark (**use code *journal50* for 50% off**).

Choose Your Flower

On the cover, the beautiful orchid was chosen to represent the journaling process. The orchid is a feminine, graceful and beautiful flower that symbolizes love, luxury, strength, rare and delicate beauty. You will see that you have all of those things and more as you complete the journal.

Now, your turn! Choose a flower that you like to represent you. Put your chosen flower in your environment throughout the year as you complete this journal. Fresh flowers will breathe new life into your environment just as you are breathing new life into your body. Flowers are beautiful just like you and flowers have to be tended to and replenished (just like you) in order for their beauty to be present.

My flower is: _____

It means: _____

I chose it because: _____

Buy your flower for yourself, hang a picture of it, ask people to give you that flower for a special occasion. Let your flower remind you that you are on a beautiful journey to love your body.

Paste or draw a picture of your flower here:

Week 1: I Like My Hair

Month: _____ Sunday Date: _____ Saturday Date: _____ Year: _____

I will treat my hair well each day this week by doing this:

_____

	One purpose or benefit of my natural hair texture	One thing that is neat about my hair	One thing I choose or refuse to do to express beauty through my hair	One good vibe/positive slogan to my hair
Sun Date:				
Mon Date:				
Tues Date:				
Wed Date:				
Thurs Date:				
Fri Date:				
Sat Date:				

If I ever feel negatively about my hair, I will do these 3 things:
- _____
- _____
- _____

I refuse to do these 3 things to harm or hate my hair:
- _____
- _____
- _____

Letter to My Hair

Dear _____:

        (positive name for my hair)

Thank you for _____
_____
_____
_____
_____
_____
_____
_____
_____
_____
_____
_____
_____
_____
_____
_____
_____

I will use these healthy products/practices to care for and honor you: _____
_____
_____
_____
_____
_____

Here is how I see you (positive picture or words):

I appreciate you most for:

Week 2: I Like My Scalp

Month: _____ Sunday Date: _____ Saturday Date: _____ Year: _____

I will treat my scalp well each day this week by doing this:

_____

	One purpose for having a scalp	One thing that is neat about a scalp	One thing I choose or refuse to do to express beauty through my scalp	One good vibe/ positive slogan to my scalp
Sun Date:				
Mon Date:				
Tues Date:				
Wed Date:				
Thurs Date:				
Fri Date:				
Sat Date:				

If I ever feel negatively about my scalp, I will do these 3 things:
- _____
- _____
- _____

I refuse to do these 3 things to harm or hate my scalp:
- _____
- _____
- _____

Letter to My Scalp

Dear _____ :

        (positive name for my scalp)

Thank you for _____

_____

_____

_____

_____

_____

_____

_____

_____

_____

_____

_____

_____

_____

_____

_____

I will use these healthy products/practices to care for and honor you: _____

_____

_____

_____

_____

_____

Here is how I see you (positive picture or words):

I appreciate you most for:

Week 3: I Like My Forehead

Month: _____ Sunday Date: _____ Saturday Date: _____ Year: _____

I will treat my forehead well each day this week by doing this:

_____

	One purpose or benefit of having a forehead	One thing that is neat about my forehead	One thing I choose or refuse to do to express beauty through my forehead	One good vibe/positive slogan to my forehead
Sun Date:				
Mon Date:				
Tues Date:				
Wed Date:				
Thurs Date:				
Fri Date:				
Sat Date:				

If I ever feel negatively about my forehead, I will do these 3 things:

- _____
- _____
- _____

I refuse to do these 3 things to harm or hate my forehead:

- _____
- _____
- _____

Letter to My Forehead

Dear _____:
(positive name for my forehead)

Thank you for _____
_____
_____
_____
_____
_____
_____
_____
_____
_____
_____
_____
_____
_____
_____
_____
_____
_____
_____
_____
_____
_____

I will use these healthy products/practices to care for and honor you: _____
_____
_____
_____
_____
_____

Here is how I see you (positive picture or words):

I appreciate you most for:

Week 4: I Like My Eyebrows

Month: _____ Sunday Date: _____ Saturday Date: _____ Year: _____

I will treat my eyebrows well each day this week by doing this:

_____

	One purpose or benefit of eyebrows	One thing that is neat about my eyebrows	One thing I choose or refuse to do to express beauty through my eyebrows	One good vibe/positive slogan to my eyebrows
Sun Date:				
Mon Date:				
Tues Date:				
Wed Date:				
Thurs Date:				
Fri Date:				
Sat Date:				

If I ever feel negatively about my eyebrows, I will do these 3 things:
- _____
- _____
- _____

I refuse to do these 3 things to harm or hate my eyebrows:
- _____
- _____
- _____

Letter to My Eyebrows

Dear _____:

       (positive name for my eyebrows)

Thank you for _____

_____

_____

_____

_____

_____

_____

_____

_____

_____

_____

_____

_____

_____

_____

_____

_____

_____

I will use these healthy products/practices to care for and honor you: _____

_____

_____

_____

_____

_____

Here is how I see you (positive picture or words):

I appreciate you most for:

Week 5: I Like My Eyelids

Month: _____ Sunday Date: _____ Saturday Date: _____ Year: _____

I will treat my eyelids well each day this week by doing this:

_____

	One purpose or benefit of eyelids	One thing that is neat about my eyelids	One thing I choose or refuse to do to express beauty through my eyelids	One good vibe/positive slogan to my eyelids
Sun Date:				
Mon Date:				
Tues Date:				
Wed Date:				
Thurs Date:				
Fri Date:				
Sat Date:				

If I ever feel negatively about my eyelids, I will do these 3 things:
- _____
- _____
- _____

I refuse to do these 3 things to harm or hate my eyelids:
- _____
- _____
- _____

Letter to My Eyelids

Dear _____:

          (positive name for my eyelids)

Thank you for _____

_____

_____

_____

_____

_____

_____

_____

_____

_____

_____

_____

_____

_____

_____

_____

_____

I will use these healthy products/practices to care for and honor you: _____

_____

_____

_____

_____

_____

Here is how I see you (positive picture or words):

I appreciate you most for:

Week 6: I Like My Eyelashes

Month: _____ Sunday Date: _____ Saturday Date: _____ Year: _____

I will treat my eyelashes well each day this week by doing this:

_____

	One purpose or benefit of eyelashes	One thing that is neat about my eyelashes	One thing I choose or refuse to do to express beauty through my eyelashes	One good vibe/positive slogan to my eyelashes
Sun Date:				
Mon Date:				
Tues Date:				
Wed Date:				
Thurs Date:				
Fri Date:				
Sat Date:				

If I ever feel negatively about my eyelashes, I will do these 3 things:
- _____
- _____
- _____

I refuse to do these 3 things to harm or hate my eyelashes:
- _____
- _____
- _____

Letter to My Eyelashes

Dear _____ :

(Positive name for my eyelashes)

Thank you for _____
_____
_____
_____
_____
_____
_____
_____
_____
_____
_____
_____
_____
_____
_____
_____
_____
_____

I will use these healthy products/practices to care for and honor you: _____
_____
_____
_____
_____
_____

Here is how I see you (positive picture or words):

I appreciate you most for:

Week 7: I Like My Eyes

Month: _____ Sunday Date: _____ Saturday Date: _____ Year: _____

I will treat my eyes well each day this week by doing this:

_____

	One purpose or benefit of eyes	One thing that is neat about my eyes	One thing I choose or refuse to do to express beauty through my eyes	One good vibe/positive slogan to my eyes
Sun Date:				
Mon Date:				
Tues Date:				
Wed Date:				
Thurs Date:				
Fri Date:				
Sat Date:				

If I ever feel negatively about my eyes, I will do these 3 things:
- _____
- _____
- _____

I refuse to do these 3 things to harm or hate my eyes:
- _____
- _____
- _____

Letter To My Eyes

Dear _____:

            (positive name for my eyes)

Thank you for _____

_____

_____

_____

_____

_____

_____

_____

_____

_____

_____

_____

_____

_____

_____

_____

_____

_____

_____

I will use these healthy products/practices to care for and honor you: _____

_____

_____

_____

_____

_____

Here is how I see you (positive picture or words):

I appreciate you most for:

Week 8: I Like My Nose

Month: _____ Sunday Date: _____ Saturday Date: _____ Year: _____

I will treat my nose well each day this week by doing this:

_____

	One purpose or benefit of a nose	One thing that is neat about my nose	One thing I choose or refuse to do to express beauty through my nose.	One good vibe/positive slogan to my nose.
Sun Date:				
Mon Date:				
Tues Date:				
Wed Date:				
Thurs Date:				
Fri Date:				
Sat Date:				

If I ever feel negatively about my nose, I will do these 3 things:
- _____
- _____
- _____

I refuse to do these 3 things to harm or hate my nose:
- _____
- _____
- _____

Letter to My Nose

Dear _____:

          (positive name for my nose)

Thank you for _____

_____

_____

_____

_____

_____

_____

_____

_____

_____

_____

_____

_____

_____

_____

_____

_____

_____

_____

I will use these healthy products/practices to care for and honor you: _____

_____

_____

_____

_____

_____

Here is how I see you (positive picture or words):

I appreciate you most for:

Week 9: I Like My Cheeks

Month: _____ Sunday Date: _____ Saturday Date: _____ Year: _____

I will treat my cheeks well each day this week by doing this:

_____

	One purpose or benefit of cheeks	One thing that is neat about my cheeks	One thing I choose or refuse to do to express beauty through my cheeks.	One good vibe/positive slogan to my cheeks
Sun Date:				
Mon Date:				
Tues Date:				
Wed Date:				
Thurs Date:				
Fri Date:				
Sat Date:				

If I ever feel negatively about my cheeks, I will do these 3 things:
- _____
- _____
- _____

I refuse to do these 3 things to harm or hate my cheeks:
- _____
- _____
- _____

Letter to My Cheeks

Dear _____:
             (Positive name for my cheeks)

Thank you for _____
_____
_____
_____
_____
_____
_____
_____
_____
_____
_____
_____
_____
_____
_____
_____
_____
_____

I will use these healthy products/practices to care for and honor you: _____
_____
_____
_____
_____
_____

Here is how I see you (positive picture or words):

I appreciate you most for:

Week 10: I Like My Lips

Month: _____ Sunday Date: _____ Saturday Date: _____ Year: _____

I will treat my lips well each day this week by doing this:
_____

	One purpose or benefit of lips	One thing that is neat about my lips	One thing I choose or refuse to do to express beauty through my lips	One good vibe/positive slogan to my lips
Sun Date:				
Mon Date:				
Tues Date:				
Wed Date:				
Thurs Date:				
Fri Date:				
Sat Date:				

If I ever feel negatively about my lips, I will do these 3 things:
- _____
- _____
- _____

I refuse to do these 3 things to harm or hate my lips:
- _____
- _____
- _____

Letter to My Lips

Dear _____ :

(positive name for my lips)

Thank you for _____

_____

_____

_____

_____

_____

_____

_____

_____

_____

_____

_____

_____

_____

_____

_____

_____

_____

_____

I will use these healthy products/practices to care for and honor you: _____

_____

_____

_____

_____

_____

Here is how I see you (positive picture or words):

I appreciate you most for:

Week 11: I Like My Ears

Month: _____ Sunday Date: _____ Saturday Date: _____ Year: _____

I will treat my ears well each day this week by doing this:

_____

	One purpose or benefit of ears	One thing that is neat about my ears	One thing I choose or refuse to do to express beauty through my ears	One good vibe/positive slogan to my ears
Sun Date:				
Mon Date:				
Tues Date:				
Wed Date:				
Thurs Date:				
Fri Date:				
Sat Date:				

If I ever feel negatively about my ears, I will do these 3 things:
- _____
- _____
- _____

I refuse to do these 3 things to harm or hate my ears:
- _____
- _____
- _____

Letter to My Ears

Dear _____:

(positive name for my ears)

Thank you for _____
_____
_____
_____
_____
_____
_____
_____
_____
_____
_____
_____
_____
_____
_____
_____
_____
_____

I will use these healthy products/practices to care for and honor you: _____
_____
_____
_____
_____
_____

Here is how I see you (positive picture or words):

I appreciate you most for:

Week 12: I Like My Complexion

Month: _____ Sunday Date: _____ Saturday Date: _____ Year: _____

I will treat my complexion well each day this week by doing this:

_____

	One purpose or benefit of having a complexion	One thing that is neat about my complexion	One thing I choose or refuse to do to express beauty through my complexion	One good vibe/positive slogan to my complexion
Sun Date:				
Mon Date:				
Tues Date:				
Wed Date:				
Thurs Date:				
Fri Date:				
Sat Date:				

If I ever feel negatively about my complexion, I will do these 3 things:
- _____
- _____
- _____

I refuse to do these 3 things to harm or hate my complexion:
- _____
- _____
- _____

Letter to My Complexion

Dear _____:
(positive name for my complexion)

Thank you for _____

_____
_____
_____
_____
_____
_____
_____
_____
_____
_____
_____
_____
_____
_____
_____
_____
_____
_____
_____

I will use these healthy products/practices to care for and honor you: _____

_____
_____
_____
_____
_____

Here is how I see you (positive picture or words):

I appreciate you most for:

Week 13: I Like My Teeth

Month: _____ Sunday Date: _____ Saturday Date: _____ Year: _____

I will treat my teeth well each day this week by doing this:

_____

	One purpose or benefit of teeth	One thing that is neat about my teeth	One thing I choose or refuse to do to express beauty through my teeth	One good vibe/positive slogan to my teeth
Sun Date:				
Mon Date:				
Tues Date:				
Wed Date:				
Thurs Date:				
Fri Date:				
Sat Date:				

If I ever feel negatively about my teeth, I will do these 3 things:
- _____
- _____
- _____

I refuse to do these 3 things to harm or hate my teeth:
- _____
- _____
- _____

Letter to My Teeth

Dear _____:
(positive name for my teeth)

Thank you for _____
_____
_____
_____
_____
_____
_____
_____
_____
_____
_____
_____
_____
_____
_____
_____
_____
_____

I will use these healthy products/practices to care for and honor you: _____
_____
_____
_____
_____
_____

Here is how I see you (positive picture or words):

I appreciate you most for:

Week 14: I Like My Smile

Month: _____ Sunday Date: _____ Saturday Date: _____ Year: _____

I will treat my smile well each day this week by doing this:

_____

	One purpose or benefit of smile	One thing that is neat about my smile	One thing I choose or refuse to do to express beauty through my smile	One good vibe/positive slogan to my smile
Sun Date:				
Mon Date:				
Tues Date:				
Wed Date:				
Thurs Date:				
Fri Date:				
Sat Date:				

If I ever feel negatively about my smile, I will do these 3 things:
- _____
- _____
- _____

I refuse to do these 3 things to harm or hate my smile:
- _____
- _____
- _____

Letter to My Smile

Dear _____:
(positive name for my smile)

Thank you for _____
_____
_____
_____
_____
_____
_____
_____
_____
_____
_____
_____
_____
_____
_____
_____
_____
_____
_____
_____

I will use these healthy products/practices to care for and honor you: _____
_____
_____
_____
_____
_____

Here is how I see you (positive picture or words):

I appreciate you most for:

Week 15: I Like My Chin

Month: _____ Sunday Date: _____ Saturday Date: _____ Year: _____

I will treat my chin well each day this week by doing this:

_____

	One purpose or benefit of a chin	One thing that is neat about my chin	One thing I choose or refuse to do to express beauty through my chin	One good vibe/positive slogan to my chin
Sun Date:				
Mon Date:				
Tues Date:				
Wed Date:				
Thurs Date:				
Fri Date:				
Sat Date:				

If I ever feel negatively about my chin, I will do these 3 things:
- _____
- _____
- _____

I refuse to do these 3 things to harm or hate my chin:
- _____
- _____
- _____

Letter to My Chin

Dear _____:

        (positive name for my chin)

Thank you for _____

_____

_____

_____

_____

_____

_____

_____

_____

_____

_____

_____

_____

_____

_____

_____

_____

I will use these healthy products/practices to care for and honor you: _____

_____

_____

_____

_____

_____

Here is how I see you (positive picture or words):

I appreciate you most for:

Week 16: I Like My Neck

Month: _____ Sunday Date: _____ Saturday Date: _____ Year: _____

I will treat my neck well each day this week by doing this:

_____

	One purpose or benefit of a neck	One thing that is neat about my neck	One thing I choose or refuse to do to express beauty through my neck	One good vibe/positive slogan to my neck
Sun Date:				
Mon Date:				
Tues Date:				
Wed Date:				
Thurs Date:				
Fri Date:				
Sat Date:				

If I ever feel negatively about my neck, I will do these 3 things:
- _____
- _____
- _____

I refuse to do these 3 things to harm or hate my neck:
- _____
- _____
- _____

Letter to My Neck

Dear _____:

       (positive name for my neck)

Thank you for _____

_____

_____

_____

_____

_____

_____

_____

_____

_____

_____

_____

_____

_____

_____

_____

I will use these healthy products/practices to care for and honor you: _____

_____

_____

_____

_____

_____

Here is how I see you (positive picture or words):

I appreciate you most for:

Week 17: I Like My Voice

Month: _____ Sunday Date: _____ Saturday Date: _____ Year: _____

I will treat my voice well each day this week by doing this:

_____

	One purpose or benefit of voice	One thing that is neat about my voice	One thing I choose or refuse to do to express beauty through my voice	One good vibe/positive slogan to my voice
Sun Date:				
Mon Date:				
Tues Date:				
Wed Date:				
Thurs Date:				
Fri Date:				
Sat Date:				

If I ever feel negatively about my voice, I will do these 3 things:
- _____
- _____
- _____

I refuse to do these 3 things to harm or hate my voice:
- _____
- _____
- _____

Letter to My Voice

Dear _____ :

               (positive name for my voice)

Thank you for _____

_____

_____

_____

_____

_____

_____

_____

_____

_____

_____

_____

_____

_____

_____

_____

_____

_____

I will use these healthy products/practices to care for and honor you: _____

_____

_____

_____

_____

Here is how I see you (positive picture or words):

I appreciate you most for:

Week 18: I Like My Arms

Month: _____ Sunday Date: _____ Saturday Date: _____ Year: _____

I will treat my arms well each day this week by doing this:

_____

	One purpose or benefit of arms	One thing that is neat about my arms	One thing I choose or refuse to do to express beauty through my arms	One good vibe/positive slogan to my arms
Sun Date:				
Mon Date:				
Tues Date:				
Wed Date:				
Thurs Date:				
Fri Date:				
Sat Date:				

If I ever feel negatively about my arms, I will do these 3 things:
- _____
- _____
- _____

I refuse to do these 3 things to harm or hate my arms:
- _____
- _____
- _____

Letter to My Arms

Dear _____ :
          (positive name for my arms)

Thank you for _____
_____
_____
_____
_____
_____
_____
_____
_____
_____
_____
_____
_____
_____
_____
_____
_____
_____
_____

I will use these healthy products/practices to care for and honor you: _____
_____
_____
_____
_____
_____

Here is how I see you (positive picture or words):

I appreciate you most for:

Week 19: I Like My Armpits

Month: _____ Sunday Date: _____ Saturday Date: _____ Year: _____

I will treat my armpits well each day this week by doing this:

_____

	One purpose or benefit of armpits	One thing that is neat about my armpits	One thing I choose or refuse to do to express beauty through my armpits	One good vibe/positive slogan to my armpits
Sun Date:				
Mon Date:				
Tues Date:				
Wed Date:				
Thurs Date:				
Fri Date:				
Sat Date:				

If I ever feel negatively about my armpits, I will do these 3 things:
- _____
- _____
- _____

I refuse to do these 3 things to harm or hate my armpits:
- _____
- _____
- _____

Letter to My Armpits

Dear _____ :

        (positive name for my armpits)

Thank you for _____
_____
_____
_____
_____
_____
_____
_____
_____
_____
_____
_____
_____
_____
_____
_____
_____
_____

I will use these healthy products/practices to care for and honor you: _____
_____
_____
_____
_____
_____

Here is how I see you (positive picture or words):

I appreciate you most for:

Week 20: I Like My Hands

Month: _____ Sunday Date: _____ Saturday Date: _____ Year: _____

I will treat my hands well each day this week by doing this:

_____

	One purpose or benefit of hands	One thing that is neat about my hands	One thing I choose or refuse to do to express beauty through my hands	One good vibe/positive slogan to my hands
Sun Date:				
Mon Date:				
Tues Date:				
Wed Date:				
Thurs Date:				
Fri Date:				
Sat Date:				

If I ever feel negatively about my hands, I will do these 3 things:
- _____
- _____
- _____

I refuse to do these 3 things to harm or hate my hands:
- _____
- _____
- _____

Letter to My Hands

Dear _____:

(positive name for my hands)

Thank you for _____

_____

_____

_____

_____

_____

_____

_____

_____

_____

_____

_____

_____

_____

_____

_____

_____

_____

I will use these healthy products/practices to care for and honor you: _____

_____

_____

_____

_____

_____

Here is how I see you (positive picture or words):

I appreciate you most for:

Week 21: I Like My Fingernails

Month: _____ Sunday Date: _____ Saturday Date: _____ Year: _____

I will treat my fingernails well each day this week by doing this:

_____

	One purpose or benefit of fingernails	One thing that is neat about my fingernails	One thing I choose or refuse to do to express beauty through my fingernails	One good vibe/positive slogan to my fingernails
Sun Date:				
Mon Date:				
Tues Date:				
Wed Date:				
Thurs Date:				
Fri Date:				
Sat Date:				

If I ever feel negatively about my fingernails, I will do these 3 things:
- _____
- _____
- _____

I refuse to do these 3 things to harm or hate my fingernails:
- _____
- _____
- _____

Letter to My Fingernails

Dear _____ :

(positive name for my fingernails)

Thank you for _____
_____
_____
_____
_____
_____
_____
_____
_____
_____
_____
_____
_____
_____
_____
_____
_____
_____

I will use these healthy products/practices to care for and honor you: _____
_____
_____
_____
_____
_____

Here is how I see you (positive picture or words):

I appreciate you most for:

Week 22: I Like My Breasts

Month: _____ Sunday Date: _____ Saturday Date: _____ Year: _____

I will treat my breasts well each day this week by doing this:

_____

	One purpose or benefit of breasts	One thing that is neat about my breasts	One thing I choose or refuse to do to express beauty through my breasts	One good vibe/positive slogan to my breasts
Sun Date:				
Mon Date:				
Tues Date:				
Wed Date:				
Thurs Date:				
Fri Date:				
Sat Date:				

If I ever feel negatively about my breasts, I will do these 3 things:
- _____
- _____
- _____

I refuse to do these 3 things to harm or hate my breasts:
- _____
- _____
- _____

Letter to My Breasts

Dear _____:

(positive name for my breasts)

Thank you for _____
_____
_____
_____
_____
_____
_____
_____
_____
_____
_____
_____
_____
_____
_____
_____
_____
_____

I will use these healthy products/practices to care for and honor you: _____
_____
_____
_____
_____
_____

Here is how I see you (positive picture or words):

I appreciate you most for:

Week 23: I Like My Back

Month: _____ Sunday Date: _____ Saturday Date: _____ Year: _____

I will treat my back well each day this week by doing this:

_____

	One purpose or benefit of a back	One thing that is neat about my back	One thing I choose or refuse to do to express beauty through my back	One good vibe/positive slogan to my back
Sun Date:				
Mon Date:				
Tues Date:				
Wed Date:				
Thurs Date:				
Fri Date:				
Sat Date:				

If I ever feel negatively about my rib cage, I will do these 3 things:
- _____
- _____
- _____

I refuse to do these 3 things to harm or hate my back:
- _____
- _____
- _____

Letter to My Back

Dear _____ :

(positive name for my back)

Thank you for _____

_____

_____

_____

_____

_____

_____

_____

_____

_____

_____

_____

_____

_____

_____

_____

_____

_____

_____

I will use these healthy products/practices to care for and honor you: _____

_____

_____

_____

_____

_____

Here is how I see you (positive picture or words):

I appreciate you most for:

Week 24: I Like My Stomach

Month: _____ Sunday Date: _____ Saturday Date: _____ Year: _____

I will treat my stomach well each day this week by doing this:

_____

	One purpose or benefit of a stomach	One thing that is neat about my stomach	One thing I choose or refuse to do to express beauty through my stomach	One good vibe/positive slogan to my stomach
Sun Date:				
Mon Date:				
Tues Date:				
Wed Date:				
Thurs Date:				
Fri Date:				
Sat Date:				

If I ever feel negatively about my stomach, I will do these 3 things:
- _____
- _____
- _____

I refuse to do these 3 things to harm or hate my stomach:
- _____
- _____
- _____

Letter to My Stomach

Dear _____ :

(positive name for my stomach)

Thank you for _____

_____

_____

_____

_____

_____

_____

_____

_____

_____

_____

_____

_____

_____

_____

_____

_____

_____

I will use these healthy products/practices to care for and honor you: _____

_____

_____

_____

_____

Here is how I see you (positive picture or words):

I appreciate you most for:

Week 25: I Like My Womb, Ovaries and Fallopian Tubes

Month: _____ Sunday Date: _____ Saturday Date: _____ Year: _____

I will treat my womb, ovaries, and/or fallopian tubes well each day this week by doing this:

_____

	One purpose or benefit of a womb, ovaries, and/or fallopian tubes	What is neat about my womb, ovaries, and/or fallopian tubes	I choose to do what with my womb, ovaries, and/or fallopian tubes	One good vibe/ positive slogan to my womb, ovaries, and/or fallopian tubes
Sun Date:				
Mon Date:				
Tues Date:				
Wed Date:				
Thurs Date:				
Fri Date:				
Sat Date:				

If I ever feel negatively about my womb, ovaries, and/or fallopian tubes, I will do these 3 things:
- _____
- _____
- _____

I refuse to do these things to harm or hate my womb, ovaries, and fallopian tubes:
- _____
- _____
- _____

Letter to My Womb, Ovaries, Fallopian Tubes

Dear _____:
(positive name for my womb, ovaries, fallopian tubes)

Thank you for _____
_____
_____
_____
_____

I will use these healthy products/practices to care for and honor you: _____
_____
_____

Here is how I see you (positive picture or words):

I appreciate you most for:

Week 26: I Like My Yoni

Month: _____ Sunday Date: _____ Saturday Date: _____ Year: _____

I will treat my yoni well each day this week by doing this:

_____

	One purpose or benefit of a yoni	One thing that is neat about my yoni	One thing I choose or refuse to do with my yoni	One good vibe/ positive slogan to my yoni
Sun Date:				
Mon Date:				
Tues Date:				
Wed Date:				
Thurs Date:				
Fri Date:				
Sat Date:				

If I ever feel negatively about my yoni, I will do these 3 things:

- _____
- _____
- _____

I refuse to do these 3 things to harm or hate my yoni:

- _____
- _____
- _____

Letter to My Yoni

Dear _____:

(positive name for yoni)

Thank you for _____

_____
_____
_____
_____
_____
_____
_____
_____
_____
_____
_____
_____
_____
_____
_____
_____
_____

I will use these healthy products/practices to care for and honor you: _____

_____
_____
_____
_____
_____

Here is how I see you (positive picture or words):

I appreciate you most for:

Week 27: I Like My Menstrual Cycle or Menopause

Month: _____ Sunday Date: _____ Saturday Date: _____ Year: _____

I will honor my menstrual cycle or menopause each day this week by doing this:

_____

	One purpose or benefit of a menstrual cycle or menopause	One thing that is neat about my menstrual cycle or about menopause	One thing I choose to do to honor AND one thing I refuse to do to dishonor my menstrual cycle or menopause	One good vibe/positive slogan to my menstrual cycle or menopause
Sun Date:				
Mon Date:				
Tues Date:				
Wed Date:				
Thurs Date:				
Fri Date:				
Sat Date:				

If I feel negatively about my menstrual cycle or menopause, I will do this:
- _____
- _____
- _____

I refuse to do these 3 things to harm or hate my menstrual cycle or menopause:
- _____
- _____
- _____

Letter to My Menstrual Cycle or Menopause

Dear _____:
(positive name for my menstrual cycle or menopause)

Thank you for _____
_____
_____
_____
_____
_____
_____
_____
_____
_____
_____
_____
_____
_____
_____
_____
_____
_____
_____

I will use these healthy products/practices to care for and honor you: _____
_____
_____
_____
_____
_____

Here is how I see you (positive picture or words):

I appreciate you most for:

Week 28: I Like My Ability To Give Birth

Month: _____ Sunday Date: _____ Saturday Date: _____ Year: _____

I will honor my present or past ability to give birth each day this week by doing:
_____

	One purpose or benefit of giving birth	One thing that is neat about my giving birth (or not)	One thing I choose or refuse to do to honor giving birth	One good vibe/ positive slogan to myself or others about giving birth
Sun Date:				
Mon Date:				
Tues Date:				
Wed Date:				
Thurs Date:				
Fri Date:				
Sat Date:				

If I ever feel negatively about giving birth, I will do these 3 things:
- _____
- _____
- _____

I refuse to do these 3 things to harm or hate my ability to give birth:
- _____
- _____
- _____

Letter to My Ability to Give Birth

Dear _____ :
(positive name for giving birth)

Thank you for _____

_____

_____

_____

_____

_____

_____

_____

_____

_____

_____

_____

_____

_____

_____

_____

I will use these healthy products/practices to care for and honor you: _____

_____

_____

_____

_____

Here is how I see you (positive picture or words):

I appreciate you most for:

Week 29: I Like My Hips

Month: _____ Sunday Date: _____ Saturday Date: _____ Year: _____

I will treat my hips well each day this week by doing this:

_____

	One purpose or benefit of hips	One thing that is neat about my hips	One thing I choose or refuse to do to express beauty through my hips	One good vibe/positive slogan to my hips
Sun Date:				
Mon Date:				
Tues Date:				
Wed Date:				
Thurs Date:				
Fri Date:				
Sat Date:				

If I ever feel negatively about my hips, I will do these 3 things:
- _____
- _____
- _____

I refuse to do these 3 things to harm or hate my hips:
- _____
- _____
- _____

Letter to My Hips

Dear _____ :
(positive name for my hips)

Thank you for _____
_____
_____
_____
_____
_____
_____
_____
_____
_____
_____
_____
_____
_____
_____
_____
_____
_____

I will use these healthy products/practices to care for and honor you: _____
_____
_____
_____
_____
_____

Here is how I see you (positive picture or words):

I appreciate you most for:

Week 30: I Like My Buttocks

Month: _____ Sunday Date: _____ Saturday Date: _____ Year: _____

I will treat my buttocks well each day this week by doing this:

_____

	One purpose or benefit of a buttocks	One thing that is neat about my buttocks	One thing I choose or refuse to do to express beauty through my buttocks	One good vibe/positive slogan to my buttocks
Sun Date:				
Mon Date:				
Tues Date:				
Wed Date:				
Thurs Date:				
Fri Date:				
Sat Date:				

If I ever feel negatively about my buttocks, I will do these 3 things:
- _____
- _____
- _____

I refuse to do these 3 things to harm or hate my buttocks:
- _____
- _____
- _____

Letter to My Buttocks

Dear _____:
  (positive name for my buttocks)

Thank you for _____

_____

_____

_____

_____

_____

_____

_____

_____

_____

_____

_____

_____

_____

_____

_____

I will use these healthy products/practices to care for and honor you: _____

_____

_____

_____

_____

_____

Here is how I see you (positive picture or words):

I appreciate you most for:

Week 31: I Like My Thighs

Month: _____ Sunday Date: _____ Saturday Date: _____ Year: _____

I will treat my thighs well each day this week by doing this:

_____

	One purpose or benefit of thighs	One thing that is neat about my thighs	One thing I choose or refuse to do to express beauty through my thighs	One good vibe/positive slogan to my thighs
Sun Date:				
Mon Date:				
Tues Date:				
Wed Date:				
Thurs Date:				
Fri Date:				
Sat Date:				

If I ever feel negatively about my thighs, I will do these 3 things:
- _____
- _____
- _____

I refuse to do these 3 things to harm or hate my thighs:
- _____
- _____
- _____

Letter to My Thighs

Dear _____:
  (positive name for my thighs)

Thank you for _____
_____
_____
_____
_____
_____
_____
_____
_____
_____
_____
_____
_____
_____
_____
_____
_____
_____

I will use these healthy products/practices to care for and honor you: _____
_____
_____
_____
_____
_____

Here is how I see you (positive picture or words):

I appreciate you most for:

Week 32: I Like My Knees

Month: _____ Sunday Date: _____ Saturday Date: _____ Year: _____

I will treat my knees well each day this week by doing this:

_____

	One purpose or benefit of knees	One thing that is neat about my knees	One thing I choose or refuse to do to express beauty through my knees	One good vibe/positive slogan to my knees
Sun Date:				
Mon Date:				
Tues Date:				
Wed Date:				
Thurs Date:				
Fri Date:				
Sat Date:				

If I ever feel negatively about my knees, I will do these 3 things:
- _____
- _____
- _____

I refuse to do these 3 things to harm or hate my knees:
- _____
- _____
- _____

Letter to My Knees

Dear _____:

(positive name for my knees)

Thank you for _____

_____

_____

_____

_____

_____

_____

_____

_____

_____

_____

_____

_____

_____

_____

_____

_____

_____

I will use these healthy products/practices to care for and honor you: _____

_____

_____

_____

_____

_____

Here is how I see you (positive picture or words):

I appreciate you most for:

Week 33: I Like My Calves

Month: _____ Sunday Date: _____ Saturday Date: _____ Year: _____

I will treat my calves well each day this week by doing this:

_____

	One purpose or benefit of calves	One thing that is neat about my calves	One thing I choose or refuse to do to express beauty through my calves	One good vibe/positive slogan to my calves
Sun Date:				
Mon Date:				
Tues Date:				
Wed Date:				
Thurs Date:				
Fri Date:				
Sat Date:				

If I ever feel negatively about my calves, I will do these 3 things:
- _____
- _____
- _____

I refuse to do these 3 things to harm or hate my calves:
- _____
- _____
- _____

Letter to My Calves

Dear _____:
(positive name for my calves)

Thank you for _____
_____
_____
_____
_____
_____
_____
_____
_____
_____
_____
_____
_____
_____
_____
_____
_____
_____

I will use these healthy products/practices to care for and honor you: _____
_____
_____
_____
_____
_____

Here is how I see you (positive picture or words):

I appreciate you most for:

Week 34: I Like My Legs

Month: _____ Sunday Date: _____ Saturday Date: _____ Year: _____

I will treat my legs well each day this week by doing this:

_____

	One purpose or benefit of legs	One thing that is neat about my legs	One thing I choose or refuse to do to express beauty through my legs	One good vibe/positive slogan to my legs
Sun Date:				
Mon Date:				
Tues Date:				
Wed Date:				
Thurs Date:				
Fri Date:				
Sat Date:				

If I ever feel negatively about my legs, I will do these 3 things:
- _____
- _____
- _____

I refuse to do these 3 things to harm or hate my legs:
- _____
- _____
- _____

Letter to My Legs

Dear _____:
(positive name for my legs)

Thank you for _____
_____
_____
_____
_____
_____
_____
_____
_____
_____
_____
_____
_____
_____
_____
_____
_____
_____
_____
_____

I will use these healthy products/practices to care for and honor you: _____
_____
_____
_____
_____
_____

Here is how I see you (positive picture or words):

I appreciate you most for:

Week 35: I Like My Toes

Month: _____ Sunday Date: _____ Saturday Date: _____ Year: _____

I will treat my toes well each day this week by doing this:

_____

	One purpose or benefit of toes	One thing that is neat about my toes	One thing I choose or refuse to do to express beauty through my toes	One good vibe/positive slogan to my toes
Sun Date:				
Mon Date:				
Tues Date:				
Wed Date:				
Thurs Date:				
Fri Date:				
Sat Date:				

If I ever feel negatively about my toes, I will do these 3 things:
- _____
- _____
- _____

I refuse to do these 3 things to harm or hate my toes:
- _____
- _____
- _____

Letter to My Toes

Dear _____:

        (positive name for my toes)

Thank you for _____

_____

_____

_____

_____

_____

_____

_____

_____

_____

_____

_____

_____

_____

_____

_____

_____

_____

_____

I will use these healthy products/practices to care for and honor you: _____

_____

_____

_____

_____

_____

Here is how I see you (positive picture or words):

I appreciate you most for:

Week 36: I Like My Toenails

Month: _____ Sunday Date: _____ Saturday Date: _____ Year: _____

I will treat my toenails well each day this week by doing this:

_____

	One purpose or benefit of toenails	One thing that is neat about my toenails	One thing I choose or refuse to do to express beauty through my toenails	One good vibe/positive slogan to my toenails
Sun Date:				
Mon Date:				
Tues Date:				
Wed Date:				
Thurs Date:				
Fri Date:				
Sat Date:				

If I ever feel negatively about my toenails, I will do these 3 things:
- _____
- _____
- _____

I refuse to do these 3 things to harm or hate my toenails:
- _____
- _____
- _____

Letter to My Toenails

Dear _____:
              (positive name for my toenails)

Thank you for _____

_____

_____

_____

_____

_____

_____

_____

_____

_____

_____

_____

_____

_____

_____

_____

_____

_____

I will use these healthy products/practices to care for and honor you: _____

_____

_____

_____

_____

_____

Here is how I see you (positive picture or words):

I appreciate you most for:

Week 37: I Like My Feet

Month: _____ Sunday Date: _____ Saturday Date: _____ Year: _____

I will treat my feet well each day this week by doing this:

_____

	One purpose or benefit of feet	One thing that is neat about my feet	One thing I choose or refuse to do to express beauty through my feet	One good vibe/positive slogan to my feet
Sun Date:				
Mon Date:				
Tues Date:				
Wed Date:				
Thurs Date:				
Fri Date:				
Sat Date:				

If I ever feel negatively about my feet, I will do these 3 things:

- _____
- _____
- _____

I refuse to do these 3 things to harm or hate my feet:

- _____
- _____
- _____

Letter to My Feet

Dear _____:

              (positive name for my feet)

Thank you for _____

_____

_____

_____

_____

_____

_____

_____

_____

_____

_____

_____

_____

_____

_____

_____

_____

_____

I will use these healthy products/practices to care for and honor you: _____

_____

_____

_____

_____

_____

Here is how I see you (positive picture or words):

I appreciate you most for:

Week 38: I Like My Skin

Month: _____ Sunday Date: _____ Saturday Date: _____ Year: _____

I will treat my skin well each day this week by doing this:

_____

	One purpose or benefit of skin	One thing that is neat about my skin	One thing I choose or refuse to do to express beauty through my skin	One good vibe/positive slogan to my skin
Sun Date:				
Mon Date:				
Tues Date:				
Wed Date:				
Thurs Date:				
Fri Date:				
Sat Date:				

If I ever feel negatively about my skin, I will do these 3 things:
- _____
- _____
- _____

I refuse to do these 3 things to harm or hate my skin:
- _____
- _____
- _____

Letter to My Skin

Dear _____ :
            (positive name for my skin)

Thank you for _____
_____
_____
_____
_____
_____
_____
_____
_____
_____
_____
_____
_____
_____
_____
_____
_____
_____
_____

I will use these healthy products/practices to care for and honor you: _____
_____
_____
_____
_____
_____

Here is how I see you (positive picture or words):

I appreciate you most for:

Week 39: I Like My Laughter

Month: _____ Sunday Date: _____ Saturday Date: _____ Year: _____

I will treat my laughter well each day this week by doing this:

_____

	One purpose or benefit of laughter	One thing that is neat about my laughter	One thing I choose or refuse to do to express beauty through my laughter	One good vibe/positive slogan to my laughter
Sun Date:				
Mon Date:				
Tues Date:				
Wed Date:				
Thurs Date:				
Fri Date:				
Sat Date:				

If I ever feel negatively about my laughter, I will do these 3 things:
- _____
- _____
- _____

I refuse to do these 3 things to mute or hate my laughter:
- _____
- _____
- _____

Letter to My Laughter

Dear _____:

        (positive name for my laughter)

Thank you for _____

_____

_____

_____

_____

_____

_____

_____

_____

_____

_____

_____

_____

_____

_____

_____

_____

I will use these healthy products/practices to care for and honor you: _____

_____

_____

_____

_____

_____

Here is how I see you (positive picture or words):

I appreciate you most for:

Week 40: I Like My Nurturing Abilities

Month: _____ Sunday Date: _____ Saturday Date: _____ Year: _____

I will honor my nurturing abilities each day this week by doing this:

_____

	One purpose or benefit of nurturing abilities	One thing that is neat about my nurturing abilities	One thing I choose or refuse to do to express beauty through my nurturing abilities	One good vibe/positive slogan to describe my nurturing abilities
Sun Date:				
Mon Date:				
Tues Date:				
Wed Date:				
Thurs Date:				
Fri Date:				
Sat Date:				

If I ever feel negatively about my nurturing abilities, I will do these 3 things:
- _____
- _____
- _____

I refuse to do these 3 things to deny or hate my nurturing abilities:
- _____
- _____
- _____

Letter to My Nurturing Abilities

Dear _____:
     (positive name for my nurturing abilities)

Thank you for _____
_____
_____
_____
_____
_____
_____
_____
_____
_____
_____
_____
_____
_____
_____
_____
_____
_____
_____

I will use these healthy products/practices to care for and honor you: _____
_____
_____
_____
_____
_____

Here is how I see you (positive picture or words):

I appreciate you most for:

Week 41: I Like My Ability to Create Beauty

Month: _____ Sunday Date: _____ Saturday Date: _____ Year: _____

I will honor my ability to create beauty each day this week by doing this:

_____

	One purpose or benefit of beauty	One thing that is neat about my ability to create beauty	One thing I choose to do to create beauty in my environment or on my personhood	One good vibe/positive slogan about my ability to create beauty
Sun Date:				
Mon Date:				
Tues Date:				
Wed Date:				
Thurs Date:				
Fri Date:				
Sat Date:				

If I ever feel negatively about my ability to create beauty, I will do these things:
- _____
- _____
- _____

I refuse to do these 3 things to devalue my ability to create beauty:
- _____
- _____
- _____

Letter to My Ability to Create Beauty

Dear _____:
  (positive name for my ability to create beauty)

Thank you for _____
_____
_____
_____
_____
_____
_____
_____
_____
_____
_____
_____
_____
_____
_____
_____
_____
_____

I will use these healthy products/practices to care for and honor you: _____
_____
_____
_____
_____
_____

Here is how I see you (positive picture or words):

I appreciate you most for:

Week 42: I Like My Circular Logic

Month: _____ Sunday Date: _____ Saturday Date: _____ Year: _____

I will honor circular logic each day this week by doing this:

_____

	One purpose or benefit of circular logic	One thing that is neat about my circular logic	One thing I choose or refuse to do to honor/dishonor circular logic	One good vibe/ positive slogan about my intellect surrounding circular logic
Sun Date:				
Mon Date:				
Tues Date:				
Wed Date:				
Thurs Date:				
Fri Date:				
Sat Date:				

If I ever think negatively about circular logic, I will do these 3 things:
- _____
- _____
- _____

I refuse to do these 3 things which devalue circular logic:
- _____
- _____
- _____

Letter to My Circular Logic

Dear _____:
   (positive name for my circular logic)

Thank you for _____
_____
_____
_____
_____
_____
_____
_____
_____
_____
_____
_____
_____
_____
_____
_____
_____
_____

I will use these healthy products/practices to care for and honor you: _____
_____
_____
_____
_____
_____

Here is how I see you (positive picture or words):

I appreciate you most for:

Week 43: I Like What Drinking Water Does For My Body

Month: _____ Sunday Date: _____ Saturday Date: _____ Year: _____

I will be prepared to drink enough water each day this week by doing this:

_____

	One purpose or benefit of drinking water	One thing that is neat about drinking water	One way drinking water helps me express beauty is:	One good vibe/positive slogan about drinking water
Sun Date:				
Mon Date:				
Tues Date:				
Wed Date:				
Thurs Date:				
Fri Date:				
Sat Date:				

If I ever struggle to drink enough water, I will do these 3 things:
- _____
- _____
- _____

I refuse to do these 3 things to devalue the importance of drinking water:
- _____
- _____
- _____

Letter to Water

Dear _____ :
      (positive name for drinking water)

Thank you for _____

_____

_____

_____

_____

_____

I will use these healthy practices to drink enough clean water: _____

_____

_____

Here is how I see you (positive picture or words):

I appreciate you most for:

Week 44: I Like My Feelings and Emotions

Month: _____ Sunday Date: _____ Saturday Date: _____ Year: _____

I will honor my feelings and emotions well each day this week by doing this:

_____

	One purpose or benefit of feelings and emotions	One thing that is neat about my feelings and emotions	One thing I choose or refuse to do to express beauty through my feelings and emotions	One good vibe/positive slogan to my feelings and emotions
Sun Date:				
Mon Date:				
Tues Date:				
Wed Date:				
Thurs Date:				
Fri Date:				
Sat Date:				

If I ever feel negatively about my feelings and emotions, I will do these 3 things:
- _____
- _____
- _____

I refuse to do these 3 things to deny or devalue my feelings and emotions:
- _____
- _____
- _____

Letter to My Feelings and Emotions

Dear _____:
  (positive name for my feelings and emotions)

Thank you for _____
_____
_____
_____
_____
_____
_____
_____
_____
_____
_____
_____
_____
_____
_____
_____
_____
_____
_____

I will use these healthy products/practices to care for and honor you: _____
_____
_____
_____
_____
_____

Here is how I see you (positive picture or words):

I appreciate you most for:

Week 45: I Like My Sexuality and Pleasure Centers

Month: _____ Sunday Date: _____ Saturday Date: _____ Year: _____

I will treat my sexuality and pleasure centers well each day this week by doing this:

_____

	One purpose or benefit of sexuality and pleasure centers	One thing that is neat about my sexuality and pleasure centers	One thing I choose or refuse to do to express beauty through sexuality and pleasure	One good vibe/positive slogan to my sexuality and pleasure centers
Sun Date:				
Mon Date:				
Tues Date:				
Wed Date:				
Thurs Date:				
Fri Date:				
Sat Date:				

If I feel guilty about my sexuality and pleasure centers, I will do these 3 things:
- _____
- _____
- _____

I refuse to do these 3 things to harm or hate my sexuality and pleasure centers:
- _____
- _____
- _____

Letter To My Sexuality and Pleasure Centers

Dear _____:
    (positive name for my sexuality and pleasure centers)

Thank you for _____
_____
_____
_____
_____
_____
_____
_____
_____
_____
_____
_____
_____
_____
_____
_____
_____
_____

I will use these healthy products/practices to care for and honor you: _____
_____
_____
_____
_____
_____

Here is how I see you (positive picture or words):

I appreciate you most for:

Week 46: I Like What Quality Sleep Does For My Body

Month: _____ Sunday Date: _____ Saturday Date: _____ Year: _____

I will have quality sleep each night this week by doing this:

_____

	One purpose or benefit of quality sleep	One thing that is neat when I get quality sleep	One way I express beauty after getting enough quality sleep	One good vibe/positive slogan about quality sleep
Sun Date:				
Mon Date:				
Tues Date:				
Wed Date:				
Thurs Date:				
Fri Date:				
Sat Date:				

If I ever feel guilty about getting quality sleep, I will do these 3 things:
- _____
- _____
- _____

I refuse to do these 3 things to infringe upon getting quality sleep:
- _____
- _____
- _____

Commitment to Get Quality Sleep

Dear _____:
       (positive name for quality sleep)

Thank you for _____
_____
_____
_____
_____
_____
_____
_____
_____
_____
_____
_____
_____
_____
_____
_____
_____

I will use these healthy products/practices to care for and honor you: _____
_____
_____
_____
_____

Here is how I see you (positive picture or words):

I appreciate you most for:

Week 47: I Like My Positive Personality

Month: _____ Sunday Date: _____ Saturday Date: _____ Year: _____

I will express my positive personality each day this week by doing this:

_____

	One purpose or benefit of a positive personality	One thing that is neat about my positive personality	I will express my positive personality by doing this	One good vibe/positive slogan about my positive personality
Sun Date:				
Mon Date:				
Tues Date:				
Wed Date:				
Thurs Date:				
Fri Date:				
Sat Date:				

If I ever feel negatively, I will do these 3 things to become positive:
- _____
- _____
- _____

I refuse to do these 3 things to devalue having a positive personality:
- _____
- _____
- _____

Letter to My Positive Personality

Dear _____:

       (name for my positive personality)

Thank you for _____

_____

_____

_____

_____

_____

_____

_____

_____

_____

_____

_____

_____

_____

_____

_____

_____

_____

_____

I will use these healthy products/practices to care for and honor you: _____

_____

_____

_____

_____

_____

Here is how I see you (positive picture or words):

I appreciate you most for:

Week 48: I Like My Brain

Month: _____ Sunday Date: _____ Saturday Date: _____ Year: _____

I will treat my brain well each day this week by doing this:

_____

	One purpose or benefit of a brain	One thing that is neat about my brain	One thing I choose or refuse to do to express beauty through my brain	One good vibe/positive slogan to my brain
Sun Date:				
Mon Date:				
Tues Date:				
Wed Date:				
Thurs Date:				
Fri Date:				
Sat Date:				

If I ever feel negatively about my brain, I will do these 3 things:
- _____
- _____
- _____

I refuse to do these 3 things to harm or hate my brain:
- _____
- _____
- _____

Letter to My Brain

Dear _____:
              (positive name for my brain)

Thank you for _____
_____
_____
_____
_____
_____
_____
_____
_____
_____
_____
_____
_____
_____
_____
_____
_____
_____
_____

I will use these healthy products/practices to care for and honor you: _____
_____
_____
_____
_____
_____

Here is how I see you (positive picture or words):

I appreciate you most for:

Week 49: I Like What Prayer Does For Me

Month: _____ Sunday Date: _____ Saturday Date: _____ Year: _____

I will pray each day this week by following this routine:

_____

	One purpose or benefit of prayer	One thing that I like about prayer	One thing I choose or refuse to do to express beauty through prayer	One good vibe/positive slogan about prayer
Sun Date:				
Mon Date:				
Tues Date:				
Wed Date:				
Thurs Date:				
Fri Date:				
Sat Date:				

If I ever feel negatively about prayer, I will do these 3 things:
- _____
- _____
- _____

I refuse to do these 3 things to minimize the importance of prayer:
- _____
- _____
- _____

Prayer for My Body

Dear _____:
      (positive name for prayer)

I pray _____
_____
_____
_____
_____
_____
_____
_____
_____
_____
_____
_____
_____
_____
_____
_____
_____
_____
_____
_____

I will use these healthy products/practices to care for and honor you: _____
_____
_____
_____
_____

Here is how I see you (positive picture or words):

I appreciate you most for:

Week 50: I Like Being Happy

Month: _____ Sunday Date: _____ Saturday Date: _____ Year: _____

I will choose to be happy each day this week by doing this:

_____

	One purpose or benefit of being happy	One thing that is neat about my being happy	One thing I choose or refuse to do to express beauty through my being happy	One good vibe/positive slogan to my being happy
Sun Date:				
Mon Date:				
Tues Date:				
Wed Date:				
Thurs Date:				
Fri Date:				
Sat Date:				

If I ever need to feel happy, I will do these 3 things:
- _____
- _____
- _____

I refuse to do these 3 things that make me unhappy:
- _____
- _____
- _____

Letter to My Happiness

Dear _____:

(positive name for happiness)

Thank you for _____

_____

_____

_____

_____

_____

_____

_____

_____

_____

_____

_____

_____

_____

_____

_____

_____

I will use these healthy practices to nurture my happiness: _____

_____

_____

_____

_____

_____

Here is how I see you (positive picture or words):

I appreciate you most for:

Week 51: I Like My Femininity

Month: _____ Sunday Date: _____ Saturday Date: _____ Year: _____

I will honor my femininity each day this week by doing this:

_____

	One purpose or benefit of femininity	One thing that is neat about my femininity	One thing I choose or refuse to do to express beauty through my femininity	One good vibe/positive slogan to my femininity
Sun Date:				
Mon Date:				
Tues Date:				
Wed Date:				
Thurs Date:				
Fri Date:				
Sat Date:				

If I ever feel negatively about my femininity, I will do these 3 things:
- _____
- _____
- _____

I refuse to do these 3 things to devalue or hate my femininity:
- _____
- _____
- _____

Letter to My Femininity

Dear _____:
   (positive name for my femininity)

Thank you for _____
_____
_____
_____
_____
_____
_____
_____
_____
_____
_____
_____
_____
_____
_____
_____
_____
_____
_____

I will use these healthy products/practices to care for and honor you: _____
_____
_____
_____
_____

Here is how I see you (positive picture or words):

I appreciate you most for:

Week 52: I Like Being A Woman

Month: _____ Sunday Date: _____ Saturday Date: _____ Year: _____

I will honor my womanhood each day this week by doing this:

_____

	One purpose or benefit of being a woman	One thing that is neat about being a woman	One thing I choose to honor or refuse to do to dishonor my womanhood	One good vibe/positive slogan about being a woman
Sun Date:				
Mon Date:				
Tues Date:				
Wed Date:				
Thurs Date:				
Fri Date:				
Sat Date:				

If I ever feel negatively about being a woman, I will do these 3 things:
- _____
- _____
- _____

I refuse to do these 3 things to devalue or hate being a woman:
- _____
- _____
- _____

Letter to My Womanhood

Dear _____:
  (positive name for my Womanhood)

Thank you for _____
_____
_____
_____
_____
_____
_____
_____
_____
_____
_____
_____
_____
_____
_____
_____
_____

I will use these healthy products/practices to care for and honor you: _____
_____
_____
_____
_____
_____

Here is how I see you (positive picture or words):

I appreciate you most for:

Reflection: I Like My Body Because . . .

- Choose 1 thing from each week, or
- Choose multiple things from 1 week and none from other weeks, or
- BEST OPTION: choose multiple things from each week.

1.	27.
2.	28.
3.	29.
4.	30.
5.	31.
6.	32.
7.	33.
8.	34.
9.	35.
10.	36.
11.	37.
12.	38.
13.	39.
14.	40.
15.	41.
16.	42.
17.	43.
18.	44.
19.	45.
20.	46.
21.	47.
22.	48.
23.	49.
24.	50.
25.	51.
26.	52.

Letter to My Body

Dear _____ :
      (positive name for my body)

Thank you for _____

_____

_____

_____

_____

_____

_____

_____

_____

_____

_____

_____

_____

_____

_____

_____

_____

_____

_____

Draw or paste a photo of your body – as is!

"For Attractive lips, speak words of kindness.
For lovely eyes, seek out the good in people.
For beautiful hair, let a child run their
fingers through it once a day.
For poise, walk with the knowledge
that you never walk alone.
People, more than things, have to be restored,
renewed, revived, reclaimed, and redeemed.
Remember, if you ever need a helping hand, you
will find one at the end of each of your arms.
As you grow older, you will discover that
you have two hands, one for helping yourself
and the other for helping others."
— Sam Levenson

About the Author

Dr. Felicia Clark, a plus-size cover model and body acceptance coach, has over 15 years coaching experience. She helps women move beyond body shame, find compatible mates, and have healthy relationships.

Dr. Clark specializes in the math and science of happiness and is a frequent media expert commenting on fat shame culture, body image, deadly beauty practices, and healthy relationships. Dr. Clark warns: "women must get beyond body shame to be happy." Look for her book, "Body Shame BS: 7 Steps to Overcome The Big Business of Low Self-Esteem" where she explains how low receptivity due to body shame impedes relationships more than lack of attractiveness or beauty compliance.

She writes for the Divorce Support Center blog and helps recent divorcees date to find fulfillment. Her clients over 50 get asked out, on average, by over 4 quality men within weeks of starting coaching.

Dr. Clark speaks to girls, college students and women throughout the United States and hosts ongoing workshops and teleseminars. Find more information at www.ebooklifecoach.com.

Look For More Products By Dr. Clark at: www.ebooklifecoach.com

"I Like My Body—The Online Interactive Journal."
Join this community to get the most out of your journal.

Books:

"Body Shame BS: 7 Secrets to Overcome The Big Business of Low Self-Esteem."

"Dating Diva: 5 Secrets To The Science of Attracting High Quality Men"

"Did Cupid Dupe Us? 10 Love Secrets To Save You From Heartbreak"

Coaching Programs:

"The 10 Commandments To Love Your Body—As Is!"

"The 10 Commandments For Gender Peace: Ending The War of The Sexes."

"The 10 Commandments For A Queen: Reclaiming Femininity in Powerful Ways."

"Beyond Body Shame BS: The Experts Weigh In."

"How To Be Attractive" (In One Day)

Live Workshops

"The Feminine Flow"

Queens that Cruise – A Workshop at Sea

"A Queen's Life"

Popular Speaking Topics
(Dr. Clark can speak to your group via SKYPE or live)

"Looks That Kill: Deadly Beauty Practices"

"Gender Politics: Hypersexualization and Emasculation Weapons of Mass Destruction"

"Dating Without Disrespect: The Science of Spotting a Compatible Mate"